SCRAPES AND SCARS

No Secrets

21 - Day Journal

I'm a survivor of childhood sexual abuse and like you for many years, I searched for an understanding of why this happened to me and how I was going to live with this pain. I've struggled for years to find hope and to be normal again. Nothing worked until I begin to seek counseling.

For the next 21 days, I will take you on a journey of healing by giving you some of the tools that helped me overcome my day to day challenges. I do not have the answers to all of your questions, however, we share the same pain. Over the years, I’ve found peace of mind by doing the things that I have listed in this journal.

Some steps may not be completed right away and it may take years to complete but don't get discouraged your on the right track of healing and that's starting the process. Many of these practices will become part of your everyday activities. Pick a time and a quiet space to sit down with me every day and just become a better you.

I hope that you find some of these steps helpful in your journey for peace of mind and healing. What I recommend to all of you is to seek professional help.

> “When the mind is pure, joy follows like a shadow that never leaves"
>
> —Buddha

Scrapes and Scars: No Secrets is a journal of Healing, Empowerment and Self-Love.

Strengthening your health and well-being with Dr. Jazz

As a mental health therapist that treats people who have experienced traumatic life events, I highly recommend trauma survivors seek professional help. It is the survivors who process and heal from traumatic experiences that own the power to define themselves and their lives rather than letting the trauma define them. Therapy sessions with someone trained to provide evidenced-based treatment for such experiences can make a meaningful difference in your life, functioning, peace of mind, and happiness. It can provide a safe space and the support you need to deal with the thoughts, emotions, and reactions that have developed as a result of the traumatic event.

One tool I find especially helpful for survivors of trauma is therapeutic journaling. Unlike typical journaling, the goals of therapeutic journaling are to reflect on one's thoughts, feelings, and behaviors related to important experiences. People who engage in therapeutic journaling often do necessary work in between therapy sessions. Reflecting and processing daily helps people to bring more insightful information to the sessions. The added insight from journaling aids a person's progress in therapy such that entries inspire introspection. This introspection gives a therapist more information about the individual's thoughts and emotions and what is hindering a person from healing. Although, I recommend therapy to process traumatic events, journaling has its own unique benefits depending on how a person is functioning. One benefit is that it allows trauma survivors to express memories that have been stuck in their minds as a result of the traumatic event. Journaling also provides a space for a person to express things they are not yet ready to discuss with anyone else. The practice may help someone identify maladaptive coping responses, unhelpful thinking patterns and behaviors, and the negative impacts on their functioning in order to change these things. Most importantly, journaling can help someone process the trauma, move their lives forward, and change their lives for the better.

The Scrapes and Scars 21-Day Journal created by Chavonne Hurdle is especially and uniquely made for survivors of trauma. The quotes are inspiring and the prompts promote reflection, engage positive thinking, and request accountability in one's healing. She has provided an opportunity for a structured therapeutic journaling experience that trauma survivors may use to their benefit.

In the Spotlight

Jasmine Melody Davis, Ph.D., P.A, affectionately known as Dr. Jazz, is a licensed therapist with a Clinical Psychology Doctorate from Fairleigh Dickinson University in New Jersey. Currently, she runs a private practice conducting therapy and assessment in Miami, Florida. Dr. Jazz treats child through adult populations, in individual, family, or couple's therapy. Her training is in multiple evidenced-based practices to treat mild to severe mental health disorders, as well as issues around dating, relationships, and life stressors. Dr. Jazz' approach is to meet people with compassion, understanding, and support while they confront and overcome their hardest and sometimes darkest fears, troubles, and truths in order to live more fulfilled and balanced lives.

In addition to running a full-time private practice, Dr. Jazz stays busy as a psychology professor and researcher. In order to extend her services to those outside of the Miami area, she currently conducts online workshops and travels for speaking engagements. She also has a podcast scheduled to air in the spring of 2019. As an African American woman, Dr. Jazz is especially passionate about fighting mental disorder stigma, advocating for people of color to get equal access to mental health services and resources, and addressing the impact socioeconomic factors have on mental health. She values the interconnectedness of humanity. Dr. Jazz believes that when you change the life of one for the better you change the lives of others, and that in order for us to be better as people we must work on the individual, communities, and society as a whole.

When Dr. Jazz is not practicing, teaching, or helping, she is dancing. She spends time loving on and being loved on by her family. She exchanges, love, ideas, great energy, and good times with an awesome group of friends and inspiring people. Dr. Jazz' current, favorite thing is walking up to a new client, who does not know who she is, and watching their face as they finally realize, she is the doctor.

Dr. Jazz

Jasmine M. Davis, Ph.D., P.A.

Clinical Psychology Fellow

(443) 320-3426

askdrjazz@gmail.com

IG @askdrjazz

"Healing doesn't mean the damage never existed. It means the damage no longer controls our lives."

-Abhay Kumar

DAY 1

Healing:
Making the decision to heal is very important. This is something that you have to want for yourself and no one else. So, are you ready to heal? If so, Why?

Why are you here?
Don't spend more than a minute thinking about the answer to this question. Just start writing and fill the space.

Do you believe you are ready to heal? If so, why now?

Healing:

DAY 1

How important is it for you to heal right now?

What do you think is the first step to healing?

DAILY REFLECTIONS

Reflecting on your thoughts, feelings, actions, and breakthroughs each day can have profound effects on your physical and mental health. You can learn from the past, be mindful of the present, and anticipate the future with a reflective practice.

I'm proud of myself today because:

I will stay committed to the healing process because:

“Life is not about waiting for
the storm to pass, it’s all
about
learning to dance in the rain”
—Vivian Greene

DAILY REFLECTIONS

One thing I learned today:

One thing I would share with others:

DAY 2

Why Me?

It is not healthy for our bodies to hold onto pain, causing distress. It is time to start dealing with the memories that have been stored deep down inside.

This stage might be the hardest. Reliving what happened is never easy, but it is necessary to move through this pain. Spend some time alone thinking about the following questions.

Why you.....if not you then who?

I used to be afraid of:

DAY 2

How will avoiding the healing process affect you?

How will you benefit from the healing process?

DAILY REFLECTIONS

Reflecting on your thoughts, feelings, actions, and breakthroughs each day can have profound effects on your physical and mental health. You can learn from the past, be mindful of the present, and anticipate the future with a reflective practice.

I'm proud of myself today because:

I will stay committed to the healing process because:

DAILY REFLECTIONS

One thing I learned today:

One thing I would share with others:

“The scars you can’t see are
the hardest to heal.”
-Raghul Raghav

DAY 3

Feeling your scars:
Remembering the feeling that you felt when it happened to you. Write down everything you feel? Close your eyes and get in touch with how you felt that day?

Do you remember how you felt before the assault?	How did you feel during the event or period of events

How did you feel after the assault/abuse was over?

DAY 3

What or who was helpful to you during and after those events? Did you seek help?

DAILY REFLECTIONS

Reflecting on your thoughts, feelings, actions, and breakthroughs each day can have profound effects on your physical and mental health. You can learn from the past, be mindful of the present, and anticipate the future with a reflective practice.

I'm proud of myself today because:

I will stay committed to the healing process because:

DAILY REFLECTIONS

One thing I learned today:

One thing I would share with others:

"Sometimes it's the smallest
decision that can change
your life forever"
—Keri Russell

DAY 4

Accepting the past:
This allows you to feel what you need to feel so you can begin to let go of the hurt and anger.
Remember acceptance is necessary and critical for healing.

What do you have to do to accept the past?

How does accepting that this happened to you makes you feel in the present moment?

Do you think it is possible for you to move forward from your hurt? Why or why not?

DAY 4

A quote or affirmation that resonates with your feelings today:

DAILY REFLECTIONS

Reflecting on your thoughts, feelings, actions, and breakthroughs each day can have profound effects on your physical and mental health. You can learn from the past, be mindful of the present, and anticipate the future with a reflective practice.

I'm proud of myself today because:

I will stay committed to the healing process because:

DAILY REFLECTIONS

One thing I learned today:

One thing I would share with others:

"Grief is in two parts. The first is loss. The second is the remaking of life."
—Anne Roiphe

No more secrets.
Most women are embarrassed to talk about it because they feel like it's their fault. Well, it's not. Talking about it gives you strength and power. Find someone to confide in and open up to them.

How does living with scars affect your everyday living?

DAY 5

How do you feel about yourself today?

Identify Your Confidant

his is someone you can confide in and turn to for support through this journey.

1. Identify your confidant.

Explain what are you doing and ask if they will play this role and accept the position as your confidant.

3. Let them know why you choose them.

Reach out to this person when you need to talk, reflect, feel, and move on.

DAY 5

My Confidant is________________________________

What I need most from this person right now is:

DAILY REFLECTIONS

Reflecting on your thoughts, feelings, actions, and breakthroughs each day can have profound effects on your physical and mental health. You can learn from the past, be mindful of the present, and anticipate the future with a reflective practice.

I'm proud of myself today because:

I will stay committed to the healing process because:

DAILY REFLECTIONS

One thing I learned today:

One thing I would share with others:

"Not everything that is faced can be changed. But nothing can be changed until it is faced"

- James Baldwin

DAY 6

The Blame game:
Many survivors blame themselves for what happened. They say things like: I should not have been there or I should not have worn that. Many people never blame the abuser for what he or she did.
FYI: This is not your burden to carry, WE did nothing wrong. Direct the blame to the abuser he or she did the unthinkable to you not the other way around. Understand that it was not your fault. PLEASE

Did you blame yourself for what happened? List at least 3 reasons why you did or did not blame yourself.

1.

2.

3.

4.

5.

6.

DAY 6

Write three reasons why it is not your fault and say them five times each in the mirror.

Did you ignore what happened in hopes that it would go away? Did it work? Why?

DAILY REFLECTIONS

Reflecting on your thoughts, feelings, actions, and breakthroughs each day can have profound effects on your physical and mental health. You can learn from the past, be mindful of the present, and anticipate the future with a reflective practice.

I'm proud of myself today because:

I will stay committed to the healing process because:

DAILY REFLECTIONS

One thing I learned today:

One thing I would share with others:

"Self-compassion is nurturing yourself with all the kindness and love you would shower on someone else you cherish"

—Dr. Debra L. Reble

DAY 7

Anger:

It is a powerful emotion. Some survivors believe that being angry is a sign of weakness, but allowing yourself to work through your true emotions is a healthy habit. The anger should be directed towards the person who deserves it the most - the abuser, a family member who didn't protect you.

Express your anger by writing a letter to your abuser. What you choose to do with this letter is up to you. You may share it, read it aloud, tear it up, keep it in a drawer...... but just the act of writing a letter to the abuser can be incredibly healing by giving you the opportunity to express your anger, hurt, shame and whatever else you may be feeling.

What did you do with the letter? Why did you choose this action?

How did you feel while writing this letter?

Read the letter out loud to yourself. What kinds of feelings does it evoke?

DAILY REFLECTIONS

Reflecting on your thoughts, feelings, actions, and breakthroughs each day can have profound effects on your physical and mental health. You can learn from the past, be mindful of the present, and anticipate the future with a reflective practice.

I'm proud of myself today because:

I will stay committed to the healing process because:

DAILY REFLECTIONS

One thing I learned today:

One thing I would share with others:

“Work on being in love with
the person in the mirror who
has been through so much
but is still standing”
—Unknown

Expressing emotions good or bad:
Expressing yourself is good for you, when you don't express yourself it allows the negative feelings to fester inside. Effectively expressing emotion allows YOU to move on from troubling experiences. Articulating how you feel can decrease stress on the body and improve your physical and mental health.

DAY 8

Identify an emotion and the feeling you have right now. What is it?
Write a list of words that can help you to express that emotion.

DAY 8

What are you feeling in your physical body? Where in the body does this feeling originate?

How do you typically express your negative emotions?

What are some ways you can choose to positively express these emotions?

DAILY REFLECTIONS

Reflecting on your thoughts, feelings, actions, and breakthroughs each day can have profound effects on your physical and mental health. You can learn from the past, be mindful of the present, and anticipate the future with a reflective practice.

I'm proud of myself today because:

I will stay committed to the healing process because:

DAILY REFLECTIONS

One thing I learned today:

One thing I would share with others:

"Holding on to anger is like
drinking poison and
expecting the other person
to die"
—Buddha

Moment of truth.
The Best Day was the moment of truth for me. In moment of truth you get to confront the person who hurt you, whether in court, on the street, a meeting with family (if it was a family member). It's empowering. No matter what they say if it is an apology, denial, sentencing day in court; it's the fact that you can say to him or her what was done to you and how you feel and felt. This is meant in an attempt to close the chapter that remained open for so long in your life. This can be helpful (but is not for everyone).

At this point, you may wish to send the letter you have written, or draft a new one to your abuser (optional). If you choose not to confront your abuser it is okay. AGAIN, this is not for everyone....You are strong

DAY 9

How will you confront your abuser? Why will you do it in this way?

What was the outcome of the confrontation?

What are your thoughts on today's moment of truth? Was this a helpful stage for you?

DAILY REFLECTIONS

Reflecting on your thoughts, feelings, actions, and breakthroughs each day can have profound effects on your physical and mental health. You can learn from the past, be mindful of the present, and anticipate the future with a reflective practice.

I'm proud of myself today because:

I will stay committed to the healing process because:

DAILY REFLECTIONS

One thing I learned today:

One thing I would share with others:

"For I will restore health to you and heal you of your wounds," says the Lord."
—Jeremiah 30:17

DAY 10

Forgiveness.

Forgiving someone who hurt you is never for them, but for you. You will never forget about what has happened to you but cleansing your soul of all the feeling of hurt is important. Forgiveness frees you to live your best life clear of bitterness, pain, resentment, and anger. Live for the today in the moment; get rid of the past, and look forward to the future.

Forgiveness:

- Is about you not the offender
- Strengthens boundaries
- Increases feelings of well-being
- Decreases feelings of victimization
- Puts you in control of your feelings
- Gives you freedom

How does the thought of forgiving your abuser make you feel?

What does it mean to forgive?
Why might this be a necessary part of the healing process?

DAILY REFLECTIONS

Reflecting on your thoughts, feelings, actions, and breakthroughs each day can have profound effects on your physical and mental health. You can learn from the past, be mindful of the present, and anticipate the future with a reflective practice.

I'm proud of myself today because:

I will stay committed to the healing process because:

DAILY REFLECTIONS

One thing I learned today:

One thing I would share with others:

“True power lies in your truth.”

- Guruji Sri Sri Poonamji

DAY 11

Forgive yourself.
Forgiveness is a gift to you, not your abuser or anyone else. It is a tool to help you lesson or eliminate the negative feelings that in your gut. Forgiving doesn't mean pretending the wrong never happened. It means making the decision to not hold yourself captive by those emotions. Remind yourself that you are doing this for you:

1. Acknowledge the abuse. Write a list of everything your abuser did to hurt you. Read it. Read it again.

2. Allow yourself to feel the emotions surrounding the abuse and the effects it has had on your life up to this point. Continue to express your feelings surrounding the actions.

3. Make a decision to not hold yourself accountable anymore. Make a choice to let go of the hurt, anger, shame, regret, and whatever else you make be feeling.

4. Letting go. Hold your hands open, feel your heart open, and let your negative emotions, thoughts and abuser go.

DAY 11

Make a list of those that you feel hurt from. These could be your abuser or abusers, people connected to the abuse, or others you have felt hurt from along the way.
Meditate (sit quietly) on those people and the feelings associated. Think of letting them go.
Draw an X through each name and feeling as you let them float out of your mind.

How do you know when you have truly forgiven someone?

DAILY REFLECTIONS

Reflecting on your thoughts, feelings, actions, and breakthroughs each day can have profound effects on your physical and mental health. You can learn from the past, be mindful of the present, and anticipate the future with a reflective practice.

I'm proud of myself today because:

I will stay committed to the healing process because:

DAILY REFLECTIONS

One thing I learned today:

One thing I would share with others:

“I eventually come to understand that harboring the anger, the bitterness and resentment towards those that hurt me, I was giving the rein of control over to them. Forgiving was not about accepting their words and deeds. Forgiving was about letting go and moving on with my life. In doing so, I had finally set myself free”

—Deerheart Wolf

DAY 12

Self Care:

Embracing the child or woman you were when it happened. Feeling compassion for yourself is important. It is okay to feel for yourself. It is a part of taking care of you.

Before being violated I used to love or enjoy…

After being violated I felt and stopped doing…….

I will allow myself to feel these emotions:

I will start doing what I loved to do before:

DAILY REFLECTIONS

Reflecting on your thoughts, feelings, actions, and breakthroughs each day can have profound effects on your physical and mental health. You can learn from the past, be mindful of the present, and anticipate the future with a reflective practice.

I'm proud of myself today because:

I will stay committed to the healing process because:

DAILY REFLECTIONS

One thing I learned today:

One thing I would share with others:

“I am not what happened to me, I am who I choose to become”

—Carl Gustav Lung

DAY 13

Self Love:
Learning to love yourself again. Treat yourself to a day that is filled with loving you?

List the top things in your life that make you feel good. There is no limit to this list. Try to fill the page

DAY 13

Choose one of those things from the list and do it! Try something new every week. Take AT LEAST an hour or more to enjoy it, read it, watch it, listen to it, play it, do it. Take note of how you feel afterwards.

How did you feel afterward or during your love yourself day?

One thing I learned today:

I can incorporate more things I enjoy into my days by:

DAILY REFLECTIONS

Reflecting on your thoughts, feelings, actions, and breakthroughs each day can have profound effects on your physical and mental health. You can learn from the past, be mindful of the present, and anticipate the future with a reflective practice.

I'm proud of myself today because:

I will stay committed to the healing process because:

DAILY REFLECTIONS

One thing I learned today:

One thing I would share with others:

“Happiness is not something ready-made. It comes from your own actions.”

Dalai Lama

Letting go and moving forward.
Holding onto the past keeps you from seeing the beauty in the present moments and opening your heart to the possibilities of the future.

What are 3 fears or feelings that you feel holds you back from moving forward? Write them inside of the balloons and watch them float away.

DAY 14

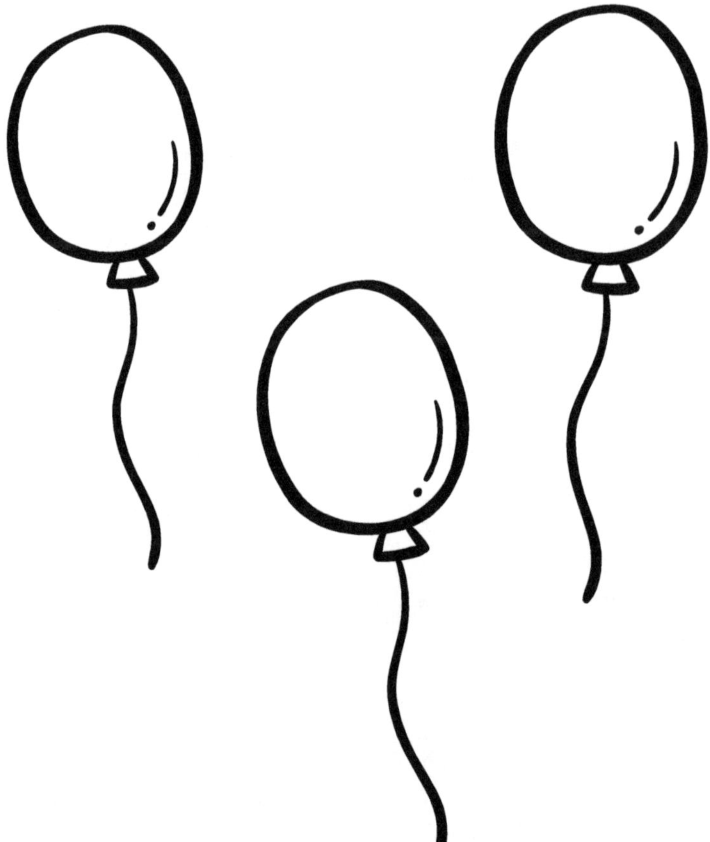

DAY 14

Once the balloons are out of sight, how does it make you feel:

By letting go of the thoughts, feelings and fears that were cluttering your heart and mind, what will you be able to do that you were not able to before?

DAILY REFLECTIONS

Reflecting on your thoughts, feelings, actions, and breakthroughs each day can have profound effects on your physical and mental health. You can learn from the past, be mindful of the present, and anticipate the future with a reflective practice.

I'm proud of myself today because:

I will stay committed to the healing process because:

DAILY REFLECTIONS

One thing I learned today:

One thing I would share with others:

"When you forgive, you in no way change the past, but you sure do change the future"
—Bernard Meltzer

DAY 15

Who are you?
After experiencing a childhood trauma like sexual abuse, I hid the little girl inside of me for years. I struggle with my own identity and lost sight of my hopes and dreams.
Today is all you. WHO ARE YOU.

If you did not experience the hurt of being abused do you think you would be a different person?

In what ways might you be different?

DAY 15

Revisit your childhood (or a happier time in your life):
Think about things from your childhood that made you happy.
List them here.

Practice finding ways to revisit your childhood.(listen to a song, play a game, watch a show, call an old friend...
How does it make you feel?
How can you adapt these moments into your adult life?

DAILY REFLECTIONS

Reflecting on your thoughts, feelings, actions, and breakthroughs each day can have profound effects on your physical and mental health. You can learn from the past, be mindful of the present, and anticipate the future with a reflective practice.

I'm proud of myself today because:

I will stay committed to the healing process because:

DAILY REFLECTIONS

One thing I learned today:

One thing I would share with others:

“The future is completely open, and we are writing it moment to moment.”
~Pema Chodron

DAY 16

Moving on.
After acknowledgement, grief, confrontation, forgiveness and letting go it is time for you to move forward with your life. Create a happy, safe space in your mind and heart where you are no longer harmed by harboring the feelings of the trauma. Take time to think about the things you are grateful for in your present life.

List things you have every day that you can be grateful for but you rarely take the time to appreciate.

List people you are grateful for. This is not just those in your life but also those that have managed to inspire and motivate you.

DAY 16

List moments in your life in which you have been proud of yourself.

List important events in your life which you learned valuable lessons.

DAILY REFLECTIONS

Reflecting on your thoughts, feelings, actions, and breakthroughs each day can have profound effects on your physical and mental health. You can learn from the past, be mindful of the present, and anticipate the future with a reflective practice.

I'm proud of myself today because:

I will stay committed to the healing process because:

DAILY REFLECTIONS

One thing I learned today:

One thing I would share with others:

“Forgiveness is not an occasional act, it is a permanent attitude”

—Dr. Martin Luther King Jr.

DAY 17

Being Mindful

Mindfulness is a way of maintaining awareness in the present moment. When you are fully present, in that moment, you are not returning to past memories or feelings. Mindfulness involves acceptance without the need or want to be somewhere else.

What does being mindful mean to you?

List 3 ways you can become more mindful:

DAY 17

Think about choices you make to go places, buy stuff, and who you spend your time with.
Are you making decisions out of habit, obligation, guilt, past emotion, or mindfulness?

How can being mindful help you to move forward?

DAILY REFLECTIONS

Reflecting on your thoughts, feelings, actions, and breakthroughs each day can have profound effects on your physical and mental health. You can learn from the past, be mindful of the present, and anticipate the future with a reflective practice.

I'm proud of myself today because:

I will stay committed to the healing process because:

DAILY REFLECTIONS

One thing I learned today:

One thing I would share with others:

“There is no passion to be found playing small in settling for a life that is less than the one you are capable of living.”

- Nelson Mandela

DAY 18

Practicing Mindfulness.

Practicing sensory and cognitive awareness is a way to bring you back from the past dwelling or future wishing and into the present moment. When you notice yourself getting caught up in worry or drifting back to past feelings, notice what is happening and remind yourself to "come back".

Cognitive Awareness Exercise #1:
Re-orient yourself in place and time by asking yourself some or all of these questions:

1. Where am I?
2. What is today?
3. What is the date?
4. What is the month?
5. What is the year?
6. How old am I?
7. What season is it?

Sensory Awareness Exercise #2:
Here's the 54321 "game".

- Name 5 things you can see in the room with you.
- Name 4 things you can feel ("chair on my back" or "feet on floor")
- Name 3 things you can hear right now ("fingers tapping on keyboard" or "tv")
- Name 2 things you can smell right now (or, 2 things you like the smell of)
- Name 1 good thing about yourself

How do you feel after practicing mindfulness activities? Which do you prefer? Are there other practices that resonate with you?

DAILY REFLECTIONS

Reflecting on your thoughts, feelings, actions, and breakthroughs each day can have profound effects on your physical and mental health. You can learn from the past, be mindful of the present, and anticipate the future with a reflective practice.

I'm proud of myself today because:

I will stay committed to the healing process because:

DAILY REFLECTIONS

One thing I learned today:

One thing I would share with others:

"Anything that's human is mentionable, and anything that is mentionable can be more manageable. When we can talk about our feelings, they become less overwhelming, less upsetting, and less scary. The people we trust with that important talk can help us know that we are not alone."

— Fred Rogers

DAY 19

Setting boundaries.

Personal boundaries define who we are by helping to create ownership and protection of ourselves. Creating boundaries is different from shutting people out. Instead they establish your personal, emotional, and physical limits. When you detach yourself from the need to understand others' behavior, thoughts and feelings, you are free to acknowledge, direct, and protect your own. Setting boundaries can be difficult in itself but is an important step in the healing process.

Exercise: Do Your Boundaries Need Work?

Ask yourself

- Do you make decisions out of feelings of obligation?
- Are you afraid to say no for fear of upsetting someone?
- Do you fill your 'free time' with the things you do not enjoy? Do you limit your suggestions when making plans?
- Are you easily persuaded to do what others want?
- Do you often keep your opinions and ideas to yourself?
- Do people often take advantage of your generosity?
- Do you maintain energy draining relationships?
- Do people look to you to solve their problems?
- Are your wants and needs unclear to you?
- Do you depend on the opinions of others?
- Say "Yes" because you are fearful of disapproval?

If you answered yes to any of these questions your boundaries may need some strengthening. How can you do that?

DAILY REFLECTIONS

Reflecting on your thoughts, feelings, actions, and breakthroughs each day can have profound effects on your physical and mental health. You can learn from the past, be mindful of the present, and anticipate the future with a reflective practice.

I'm proud of myself today because:

I will stay committed to the healing process because:

DAILY REFLECTIONS

One thing I learned today:

One thing I would share with others:

"We cannot have a world where everyone is a victim. "I'm this way because my father made me this way. I'm this way because my husband made me this way." Yes, we are indeed formed by traumas that happen to us. But then you must take charge, you must take over, you are responsible."

— Camille Paglia

DAY 20

Creating happiness.
Can you ever experience feelings of true happiness again? The answer to that is YES! Attempting to block out the past experiences using positive coping strategies like taking a time out when feeling down, deep breathing, and accepting laughter. Now that you have opened yourself up to feeling and letting go of the past, it is time to welcome happiness and joy back in.

What does happiness mean to you?

When was the last time you were truly happy? What were you happy about? Why?

DAY 20

List 3 things that make you happy and why they make you happy. (music, reading, sports, dinners out, certain people, career, etc.)

How will you welcome these things into your life?

DAILY REFLECTIONS

Reflecting on your thoughts, feelings, actions, and breakthroughs each day can have profound effects on your physical and mental health. You can learn from the past, be mindful of the present, and anticipate the future with a reflective practice.

I'm proud of myself today because:

I will stay committed to the healing process because:

DAILY REFLECTIONS

One thing I learned today:

One thing I would share with others:

“Trauma is personal. It does not disappear if it is not validated. When it is ignored or invalidated the silent screams continue internally heard only by the one held captive. When someone enters the pain and hears the screams healing can begin.”

— Danielle Bernock

DAY 21

Living life by design.
Taking back control over your life and emotions allows you space to live intentionally. The self- sabotage and victimization are also a thing of your past. When living life by design you make the choice moment after moment and day after day to be true to yourself, live life according to your values, and to make your goals a priority.

What are qualities about yourself that you would like to improve?

What is one long term goal you will set for yourself?

List two steps that will help you to reach your goal.

FINAL REFLECTION

Now that we reached the end write down your own thoughts, goals, and strategies that can help someone else get through their struggles with trauma. What have you learned about yourself and the healing process by working through the transformation? What is your biggest takeaway?

FINAL REFLECTION

Now that we reached the end write down your own thoughts, goals, and strategies that can help someone else get through their struggles with trauma. What have you learned about yourself and the healing process by working through the transformation? What is your biggest takeaway?

FINAL REFLECTION

Now that we reached the end write down your own thoughts, goals, and strategies that can help someone else get through their struggles with trauma. What have you learned about yourself and the healing process by working through the transformation? What is your biggest takeaway?

FINAL REFLECTION

Now that we reached the end write down your own thoughts, goals, and strategies that can help someone else get through their struggles with trauma. What have you learned about yourself and the healing process by working through the transformation? What is your biggest takeaway?

FINAL REFLECTION

Now that we reached the end write down your own thoughts, goals, and strategies that can help someone else get through their struggles with trauma. What have you learned about yourself and the healing process by working through the transformation? What is your biggest takeaway?

FINAL REFLECTION

Now that we reached the end write down your own thoughts, goals, and strategies that can help someone else get through their struggles with trauma. What have you learned about yourself and the healing process by working through the transformation? What is your biggest takeaway?

FINAL REFLECTION

Now that we reached the end write down your own thoughts, goals, and strategies that can help someone else get through their struggles with trauma. What have you learned about yourself and the healing process by working through the transformation? What is your biggest takeaway?

FINAL REFLECTION

Now that we reached the end write down your own thoughts, goals, and strategies that can help someone else get through their struggles with trauma. What have you learned about yourself and the healing process by working through the transformation? What is your biggest takeaway?

FINAL REFLECTION

Now that we reached the end write down your own thoughts, goals, and strategies that can help someone else get through their struggles with trauma. What have you learned about yourself and the healing process by working through the transformation? What is your biggest takeaway?

FINAL REFLECTION

Now that we reached the end write down your own thoughts, goals, and strategies that can help someone else get through their struggles with trauma. What have you learned about yourself and the healing process by working through the transformation? What is your biggest takeaway?

FINAL REFLECTION

Now that we reached the end write down your own thoughts, goals, and strategies that can help someone else get through their struggles with trauma. What have you learned about yourself and the healing process by working through the transformation? What is your biggest takeaway?

CPSIA information can be obtained
at www.ICGtesting.com
Printed in the USA
BVHW091722150419
545554BV00022B/614/P

9 781939 665904